The Children Get a Rabbit

by Rob Hip

illustrated by Barry Mullins

Core Decodable 54

McGraw Hill Education

Bothell, WA • Chicago, IL • Columbus, OH • New York, NY

MHEonline.com

Send all inquiries to:
McGraw-Hill Education
8787 Orion Place
Columbus, OH 43240

ISBN: 978-0-02-135451-1
MHID: 0-02-135451-0

Printed in Canada.

9 10 11 12 KOD 24

Dad and the children plan a trip.
They get in a truck.

They see an animal with a banana.

They see big pandas.

They pet a soft rabbit.
"Dad, can I adopt him?" asks Ellen.

Dad and Ellen get melon.

The rabbit has a carrot.

The children and Dad get in the truck.
They had a fun trip!